Is Daddy a HERO?

illustrated by Phyllis Stewart

by Sydney & Megan Carson

Copyright

Dedication

Sydney & Megan would like to dedicate this book to all of the kids in the world who have a Dad in the military. We think he is a HERO!

A Note From The Author's Daddy

It was Sydney and Megan's idea to write this book to help all military children around the world realize that their parents are true HEROES. Although they were not even born yet when I was in the military, they have heard many stories about their Daddy. They have seen several of their friends struggle with their parents being deployed around the world and wanted to do something to help. Not only do they want their friends to realize how special their military Moms and Dads are, they want everyone to realize this. I am so proud of my little girls and hope their story helps lift the spirits of our military children, and helps them see their parents as the true HEROES that they are!

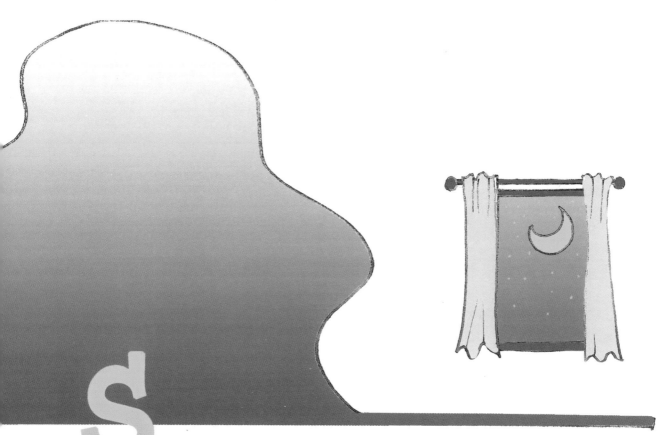

Sydney and Megan had just crawled into their beds for the night when their Daddy gave them each a kiss on the forehead and said, "Love you! Sleep tight!"

"Good night, Daddy," Sydney said.

"See you in the morning," Megan said in a soft voice.

A few minutes had gone by and Megan quietly said, "Sydney, I am a little sad!"

"Oh, Megan, we can play in the morning ... now get some sleep!" Sydney grumbled.

Megan quickly responded "NO! I heard Mommy and Daddy talking this morning and Mommy looked sad."

"Why did she look sad?" Sydney asked curiously.

"Well, Daddy gave Mommy a big hug and said that he wouldn't be gone for long," Megan said with a tear in her eye.

"Why would Daddy say this? Is he going somewhere?" Megan whimpered.

Sydney thought to herself for a moment and added, "I did hear my teacher tell our principal that he was going back to, I think AFGANAMASTAN? I think he is leaving in a few weeks!"

There was a long pause ... ...

"I sure did miss Daddy the last time he was there," cried Megan.

"I did too, Meggie" whispered Sydney.

Megan crawled back into her bed and they were both silent.

Sydney was just about asleep when Megan yelled out "Is Daddy a HERO?"

"I, I, I, think so ...   Why?" Sydney asked.

"I heard my teacher say that MY Daddy is a HERO!" Megan said with a big smile on her face.

"Is a hero kind of like the President of the United States?"
Megan asked with her head tilted to the side.

Sydney quickly responded "A hero is kind of like . . . . well . . . . .
I guess the President . . . ."

Just then she had an idea. "Come with me, Meggie," Syd said
with a twinkle in her eye.

They both tiptoed past their parent's room and down the hall to the computer in the TV room.

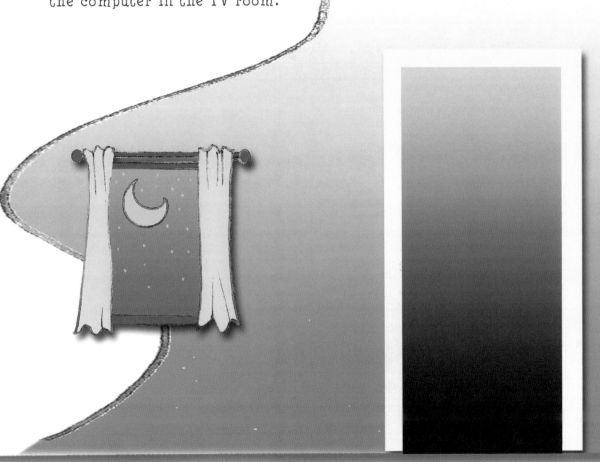

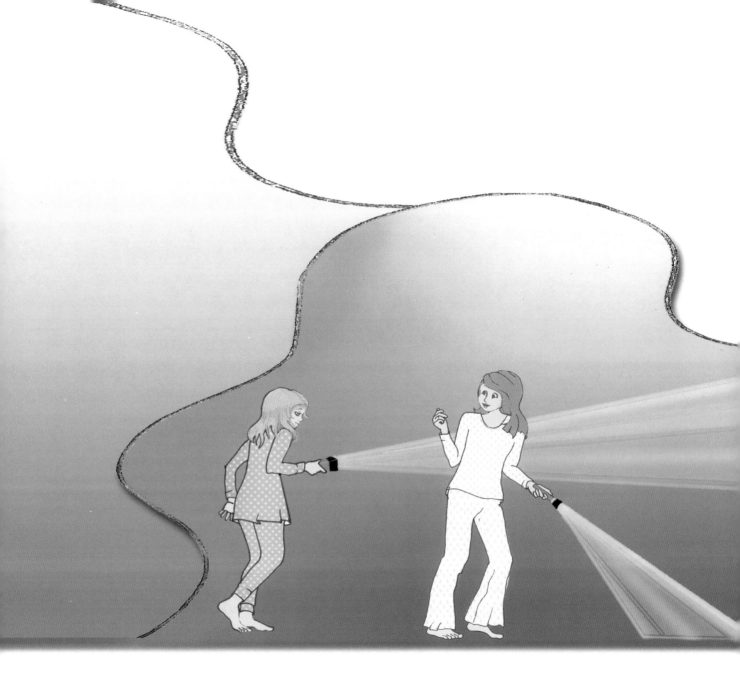

hero (hir′ō, hē′rō′) n., pl.
-roes [L heros < Gr]
pronunciation: hi ro 🔊
1.Ordinary people who do
extra-ordinary things.

Sydney whispered, "I learned how to Google stuff in school . . . all you have to do is type "H-E-R-O" and it magically appears."

Megan could hardly get the words out of her mouth, "What does it say?"

Very slowly Sydney read:

hero (hir′ō, hē′rō′) n., pl. -roes [L heros‹ Gr]

pronunciation: <u>hi</u> ro

1.Ordinary people who do extra-ordinary things.

They both stared at each other and at the same time they whispered, "WOW!"

Megan slapped her hand on her knee and asked, "What in the world does that mean?"

Sydney had a smile from ear to ear and said, "It means that Daddy is very SPECIAL, Megan."

Sydney elbowed Megan and said, "Watch this!"

She typed "M-I-L-I-T-A-R-Y" and began reading in amazement, "The military is made up of brave men and women who are part of either the Army, Air Force, Navy, Marines, Coast Guard, or National Guard and are unselfish and faithful. They do their best to protect our country so that all Americans can sleep in peace at night."

Just then they heard a noise from their parents room and thought it was best to quietly get back in their beds.

Both Megan and Sydney had many thoughts racing through their heads. They both lay silently in their beds for what seemed like an hour until Megan whispered, "I know Daddy is a great Daddy, but does he protect other people besides you and me, Syd?"

Sydney quickly replied, "Yes, Megan, he does!"

They both stared at each other with huge smiles on their faces. "You mean Daddy does what he does so that other little boys and girls can sleep in peace?" Megan proudly asked.

Syd replied, "It has to be true, the computer knows everything!"

"In the morning I am going to tell Daddy that I am soooo proud of him! He's a H E R O!!!! He's our H E R O!!!!" Megan said. "He is very special and I love him very much!"

"Me too, Meggie, me too!" Sydney replied. They both fell asleep peacefully thinking happy thoughts about their Daddy.

17

   Both girls got a good night sleep and woke up to the smell of
their Daddy making pancakes. They ran into the kitchen to give him
the biggest hug in the world.

   Megan and Sydney did not want to let go, but their Daddy said
that he needed to have a family meeting. Even though they knew
what he wanted to talk about, they were still a little sad. Their
Daddy explained that he had to leave for a few months with the
military, and that he would miss them very much.

   Megan winked her eye at Sydney and smiled while saying, "We
know all about the military and we are so proud of you, Daddy . . . you
are a hero . . . you are our HERO!!!!"

www.SoldiersAngels.org
Heroes are waiting for adoption.